T0095219

A PROVERBIAL SOUP

CAROL CADENAS

authorHOUSE®

AuthorHouse™
1663 Liberty Drive
Bloomington, IN 47403
www.authorhouse.com
Phone: 1-800-839-8640

Published by AuthorHouse   03/09/2012

ISBN: 978-1-4685-4287-5 (sc)
ISBN: 978-1-4685-4286-8 (e)

Library of Congress Control Number: 2012901095

Any people depicted in stock imagery provided by Thinkstock are models,
and such images are being used for illustrative purposes only.
Certain stock imagery © Thinkstock.

This book is printed on acid-free paper.

DEDICATION

This book is dedicated to God for loving me enough to design and create me in all simplicity and intricacy to live fully and serve along the way with no regrets while leaving a legacy of embrace and love for humankind while we, the world, still strive to make it closer to the intended paradise, yet not comfortable enough to suppress our yearning for the eternal home He's prepared for us, His adopted children.

Secondly, I dedicate this book to both my parents and grandparents for directly and indirectly blessing me with their intricate DNA along with the numerous lessons learned in all along the way. My paternal grandmother for her intentional embrace to empower me for life! I also include the great men and contributors in my life, my former husband, Scott, and our two handsome and high-energy boys for the numerous opportunities to love, receive love, and learn so much along the way in _all_!

Last, but not least, I'm grateful to you for joining me in friendship as you support these writings of mine which have only been a revelation of a few years traveled in the journey with the Man, the Creator of it all! I'm thankful for the creation of you!

TABLE OF CONTENTS

Chapter 1
WISDOM

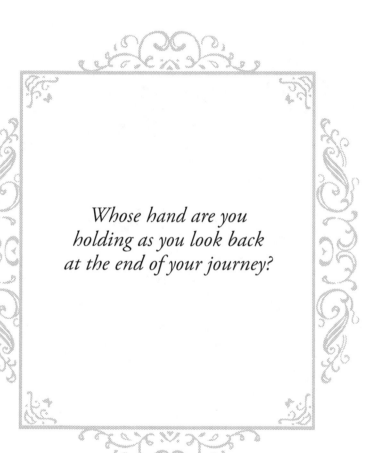

*Whose hand are you
holding as you look back
at the end of your journey?*

Why should it be easier to trust the teachings of man than the Creator of it all?

Where is wisdom treasured, in the mouth of the homeless or the corporate executive?

By recognizing one's ignorance, the doors of knowledge are opened.

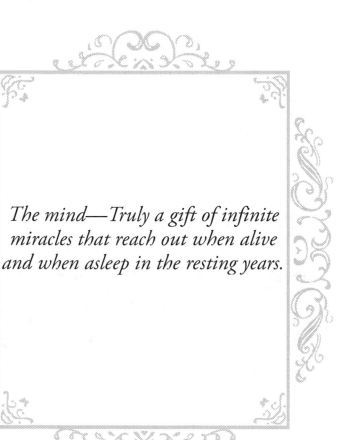

The mind—Truly a gift of infinite miracles that reach out when alive and when asleep in the resting years.

Chapter 2
THANKFULNESS AND EMBRACE

Every day we live is a testimony to God's abundant grace, mercy, and promise in His perfect love for if it's a bad day, we see His victories on our behalf; if it's a good day, we see His abundant provisions. In it all, He's present to rescue or provide.

Let me see what's in your donation,
and I will tell you where your
treasure is.

*If thankfulness brings joy to God,
why must we strive in turning off
what by nature brings us joy if we're
perfectly created in His image? Is
dancing any less holy than painting
before God? Is embracing the
plethora of cultures any less holy
than feeding the needy of the same?*

Chapter 3
HUMANITY IN
BEAUTY

Is the jaguar any less by engaging
fully in its exotic beauty and gifts?

*If we're all created in God's image
and likeness, must we persist in
judging the design of His fingers?*

When God, the Creator, delights in you, whose approval do you need?—

Tell me whom you walk with,
and I will tell you who you are.

A friend gives the heart, hands, knees in prayer, and a warm smile in any true situation.

*A genuine compliment reaches
deeper than a thousand words.*

Better it is to give a hug in friendship than give a hug to gain a friend.

Let's let humanity indeed show the wisdom accrued in thousands of years.

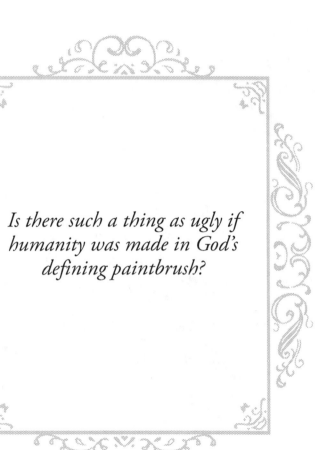

Is there such a thing as ugly if humanity was made in God's defining paintbrush?

Ladies, head up high. Are you dressed up in honor, glamour, sweetness, compassion, and valor, or regally dressed for vanity alone?

Majestic things happen when women are gathered in love to solidify and empower the present and future while embracing the truth of our past.

Low self-esteem may give us the right to diminish, underestimate, hold back, and limit our inner power and its fruits, but hatred, selfishness, and envy promotes these against others.

*The power of a woman lies in
the essential recognition to care,
empower, and rejoice in the process
no matter the cost. It was so
that God, our Creator, designated
the care of His son, Jesus Christ,
to a woman of awareness and
virtuous humility.*

The hands of a man—The strength to caress, hold, protect, secure, provide, receive, and pass on

Gentlemen, rise up. Are you cavaliers for honor, or goods of conquest?

Give away smiles each day, after all they are free; it might just be the only gift that saves a life.

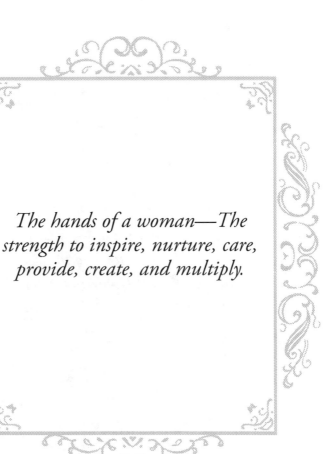

The hands of a woman—The strength to inspire, nurture, care, provide, create, and multiply.

*A date in relationships—the
intent to make it memorable
or the wondering of
what-good-could-this-person-be?*

*Love—The truest and deepest gift
a heart can give!*

The smiling for a diamond becomes a long-lasting grin in the course of the years committed to wholesomeness.

Elegance—Simplicity, Polish,
Kindness, Essence, Confidence.

A man needs to be defined as an operator for marriage . . . he needs to fully understand and be committed to the type of navigational or transportation utility he will handle. It is to say, the simpler the utility, the simpler to handle . . . a canoe cannot do what a cruise ship was designed to do.

A woman needs to be defined as a nurturer for marriage . . . she needs to fully understand and be committed to the type of gift she will care for and develop. The woman is gifted at shifting from caring for a sweet infant to being the strong polished and luscious beam lifting her man up to higher ground.

*The man who wants a strong
spiritual woman needs to fully
understand the profound ambition
and care need she entails; therefore,
she cannot be rushed, compared, cut,
and much less, displayed indecently.
Otherwise diamonds would not be
so sought after and expensive . . . the
handling of diamonds is for many,
but the displaying of their
full potential is for experts
in the field only.*

Chapter 4
PROFESSIONALISM

Even the juggler in his expertise knows to let go of what's in his hands to perform in excellence.

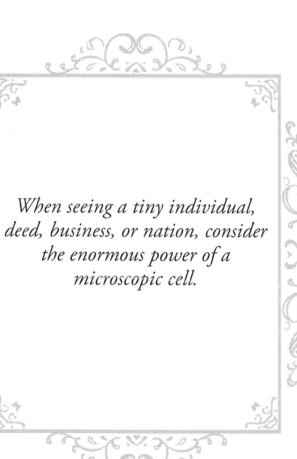

*When seeing a tiny individual,
deed, business, or nation, consider
the enormous power of a
microscopic cell.*

The essence of true conscience is the determining factor of a prosperous nation.

Courage is like an intense workout with great rewards, but complacency is like eating a box of donuts a day.

Believe. Endure. Persevere. Reap. Share.—The should-be ultimate goal of any professional in any field and of any age.

When it comes to music in children, is it better to structure it in the efforts of discipline or to encourage the freedom of its expression?

Valiant—Better be known for the courage to do what's right and needed rather than the skills of fighting.

Diligence—The conscientious application of the Majestic teachings in our every day life for it will surpass ALL mundane concerns!

Time—Your time is the existence of what and in what character?

Comfort—A double-edge sword for it's needed, yet it can cut off your opportunities of growth.

Chapter 5
DUTY

If the whole universe and the force of nature within are God's own creation and gift to man, why discard the command of our care for it?

Patriotism is the essence of recognizing unselfishly one nation's riches of all sources to be stimulated not manipulated.

*Unite, educate, and resolve must be
the perpetual burning flame
in our soul.*

The look in a child's eyes is innocence and love, so let's dive in a holy cause by surpassing any limitation to impact them perpetually.

One act of courage surpasses 1,000 mundane acts.

Impact a child in the moment for who knows when and if one will have that gift again.

If everyone accomplishes an act of courage a day, the world would appear to be paradise.

Forgive. Teach. Demonstrate. Encourage. Send.—The should-be recipe in our hearts for all.

The higher the leadership, the higher the calling to responsibility for the ones who follow.

Can you imagine the power expressed in the world and the joys in the heavens if every state or nation had an agreed yearning heart to build not destroy?

If we talk about social justice must we bring down the higher income levels or must we strive decently and earnestly for the lower income levels to rise up to more?

The human body is perfectly designed and created in His image and likeness. Every part of the body stands secured and operates in harmony for the common good of the living organism. Why must we strive in bringing down any part of the body of Christ, His bride? As any part hurts, correct and/or heal it, let us not condemn or cut it off.

Chapter 6
EMPOWERMENT

One's circumstances do not define one's identity or future, only the challenges to overcome.

When seeing a tiny individual, deed, business, or nation, consider the enormous power of a microscopic cell.

Engaging in a spiritual dive is truly the best adrenaline rush.

God, the Majestic Creator, grins when you acknowledge impossible things in your life!

*As we travel in the journey of life
what do we identify within all our
surroundings? Perhaps a boulder, a
highway, a legend, a scripture, or the
deep creation within us gifted by the
Artist of artists. It's never too
late to look within intentionally
and as intensely as possible.*

To drive a sports car in higher speed and intricate terrain, is to get a satisfying appreciation for its making.

Better is to not just smell the flowers in the path of our journey, we may be in a desert. What is your desert, spring, or valley offering you?

What makes us more humble like Jesus, the quiet surrendering of our all including the will and the gifts we're designed with; or in the exuberant acknowledgement of the plethora and complexity of our design?

Choice is the power to undo, dwell, or multiply.

*Fear—The most undesired enemy
in and to humanity.*

Ambition—Does a holy ambition strip off one's intricate and perfect overall design?

Anger—If anger were a nuclear weapon, wouldn't we want it to saturate all around with greatness? Anger when in check can ignite wonders!

Sorrow—It can wake up the truest recipe for what we truly desire or need in the moment and future while embracing the richness of the loss

Crying—The God-given gift of rinsing the soul.

Imagination—Empowering resourcefulness for execution not mental or visual wondering.

Is the chameleonizing to every need or individual more of a multiple personality symptom or the strength to dispose of our routine and comfortable design to meet our or someone else's needs and dreams?

What makes us a better son or daughter, the surrendering of self for the parent's sake or the empowering of the parent's growth in whichever way they will learn more? After all, isn't independence what's given to a child to learn how to get up from a fall, walk, and run under supervision?

Chapter 7
SCRIPTURES

There are so many Biblical passages of influence in my life, and the following, a small representation of such.

<u>Wisdom</u>:

Exodus 31:3, 1 Kings 4:29,
1 Kings 5:12, 1 Kings 10:8,
2 Chronicles 1:10, 2 Chronicles 1:1,
and Ecclesiastes 5:15

<u>Thankfulness and Embrace</u>:

Leviticus 7:12, 1 Corinthians 10:30, Colossians 2:7, 1 Timothy 1:15, Romans 11:15, Psalm 89:47, Ephesians 2:15, and Hebrews 2:14

Humanity in Beauty:

Genesis 1:26, Genesis 1:27, James 3:9, Hebrews 4:13, and Psalm 139:13

Professionalism:

Romans 5:4, 2 Thessalonians 3:5, Hebrews 12:1, James 1:3, 1 Peter 2:15, 1 Chronicles 17:2, Hebrews 6:11, and Luke 9:62

<u>Duty</u>:

*2 Kings 11:5, 7, Nehemiah 7:3,
Ecclesiastes 12:13, Luke 17:1,
1 Samuel 16:22, Luke 9:62,
Luke 12:35, Romans 12:3,
1 Corinthians 3:9, 1 Corinthians
12:5, 2 Corinthians 9:12, and
1 Timothy 1:12*

Empowerment:

Deuteronomy 9:29, Job 9:4, 1
Timothy 1:12, Psalm 20:6, Psalm
77:14, Proverbs 3:27, Romans
15:13, Philippians 3:21